Your Five Senses and Your Sixth Sense

Sight

Connor Dayton

PowerKiDS press

New York

Published in 2014 by The Rosen Publishing Group, Inc.
29 East 21st Street, New York, NY 10010

First Edition

Editor: Jennifer Way
Book Design: Kate Vlachos
Photo Researcher: Katie Stryker

Photo Credits: Cover Adam Hester/Stockbyte/Getty Images; p. 4 Cherry-Merry/Shutterstock.com; p. 7 robert_s/Shutterstock.com; p. 8 Jane McIlroy/Shutterstock.com; pp. 11, 24 (reflects) Blend Images/Shutterstock.com; p. 12 James Laurie/Shutterstock.com; pp. 15, 24 (contacts, nerves) © iStockphoto/Thinkstock; p. 16 Monkey Business Images/Shutterstock.com; p. 19 Jeroen van den Broek/Shutterstock.com; p. 20 © Digital Vision/D. Anschutz/Thinkstock; p. 23 wavebreakmedia/Shutterstock.com.

Library of Congress Cataloging-in-Publication Data

Dayton, Connor, author.
 Sight / by Connor Dayton. – First edition.
     pages cm. — (Your five senses and your sixth sense)
 Includes index.
 ISBN 978-1-4777-2850-5 — ISBN 978-1-4777-2851-2 (pbk.) —
ISBN 978-1-4777-2854-3 (6-pack)
 1. Vision—Juvenile literature. I. Title.
 QP475.7.D39 2014
 612.8′4—dc23
                            2013016412

Manufactured in the United States of America

CPSIA Compliance Information: Batch #W14PK3: For Further Information contact Rosen Publishing, New York, New York at 1-800-237-9932

CONTENTS

4

Sight is one of your five senses. Sight uses your eyes and your brain.

Your eyes take in light. Light looks white. Light is made of different colors mixed together.

7

8

Light moves in waves.
Sometimes these waves bend.
Then you see the colors that
make up light.

Light **reflects** off of mirrors. This is why you see yourself! The first mirrors were made from a shiny black rock called obsidian.

Images enter your eyes. **Nerves** in your eyes send images to your brain. Your brain tells you what you see.

Some images play tricks on your eyes. Do you see a vase? Do you see two faces?

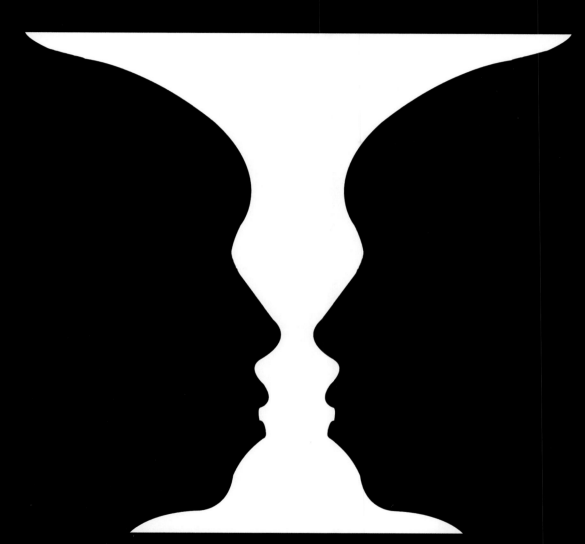

15

People with poor eyesight wear glasses. Some people wear **contact lenses** instead.

Blind people cannot see. The top cause of blindness in older people is cataracts. These form when the eye's lens gets cloudy.

Taking care of your sight is smart. Keeping your eyes safe is one thing you can do.

You use sight to do things every day. You are using sight to read this book!

WORDS TO KNOW

contact lens

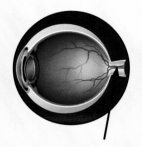

nerve

reflect

WEBSITES

Due to the changing nature of Internet links, PowerKids Press has developed an online list of websites related to the subject of this book. This site is updated regularly. Please use this link to access the list:
www.powerkidslinks.com/yfsyss/sight/

INDEX